Basic English Grammar for Kids

 2

Section 1　Vowels （母音ってなあに？）

Write the missing letters.（アルファベットを書いて電車を完成させよう!）

Uppercase（大文字）

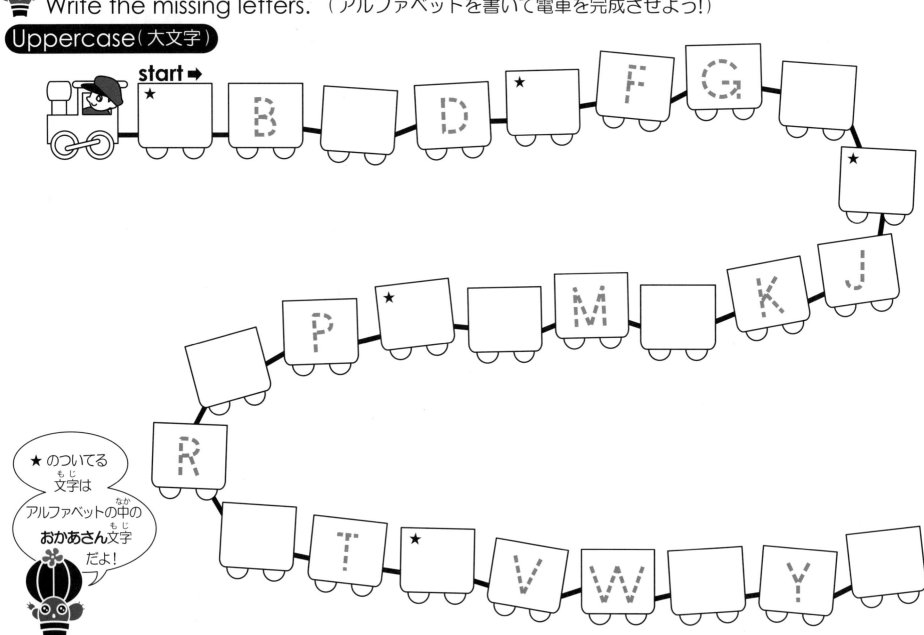

★ のついてる
文字は
アルファベットの中の
おかあさん文字
だよ!

アルファベット 26 文字の中で下の5つの文字はお母さん文字（母音）だよ。覚えてね。

 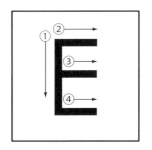 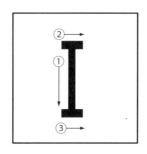 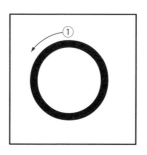 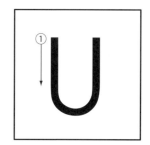

 Write the letters on the dotted lines. （点線の上に文字を書こう！）

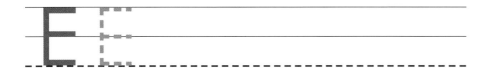 

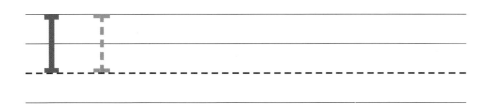

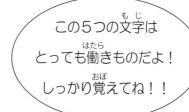

この5つの文字は
とっても働きものだよ！
しっかり覚えてね！！

-3-

Write the missing letters. （アルファベットを書いて電車を完成させよう！）

Lowercase（小文字）

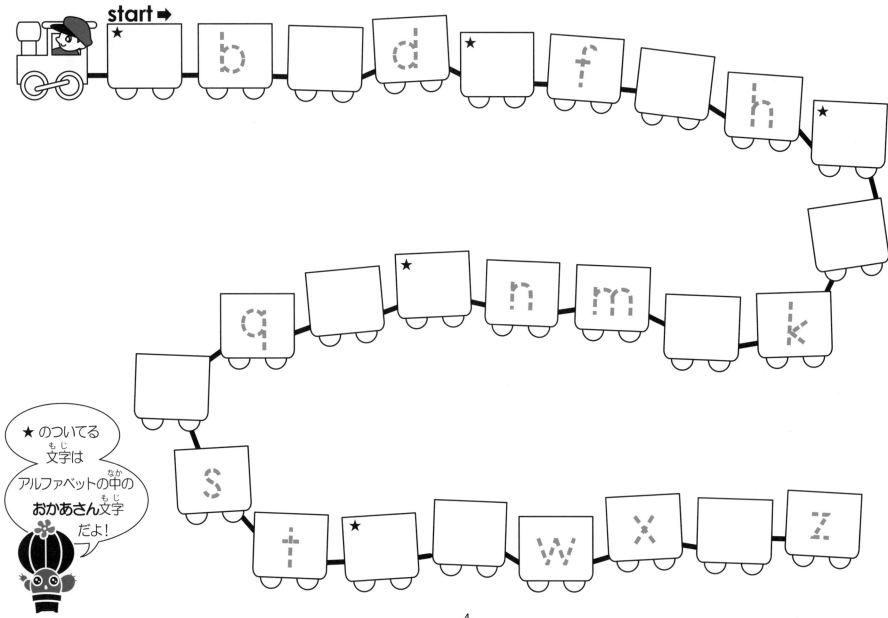

★ のついてる
文字は
アルファベットの中の
おかあさん文字
だよ！

アルファベット26文字の中で下の5つの文字はお母さん文字（母音）だよ。覚えてね。

  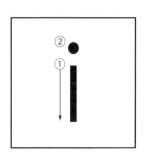 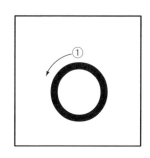 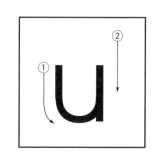

 Write the letters on the dotted lines. （点線の上に文字を書こう！）

a

e

i

o

u

覚えるヒント
『ア』『イ』『ウ』『エ』『オ』とも
読めるよ！

-5-

Circle the vowels below. （お母_{かあ}さん文字_{もじ}（母音_{ぼいん}）を見_みつけて全部_{ぜんぶ} ◯ をつけよう！）

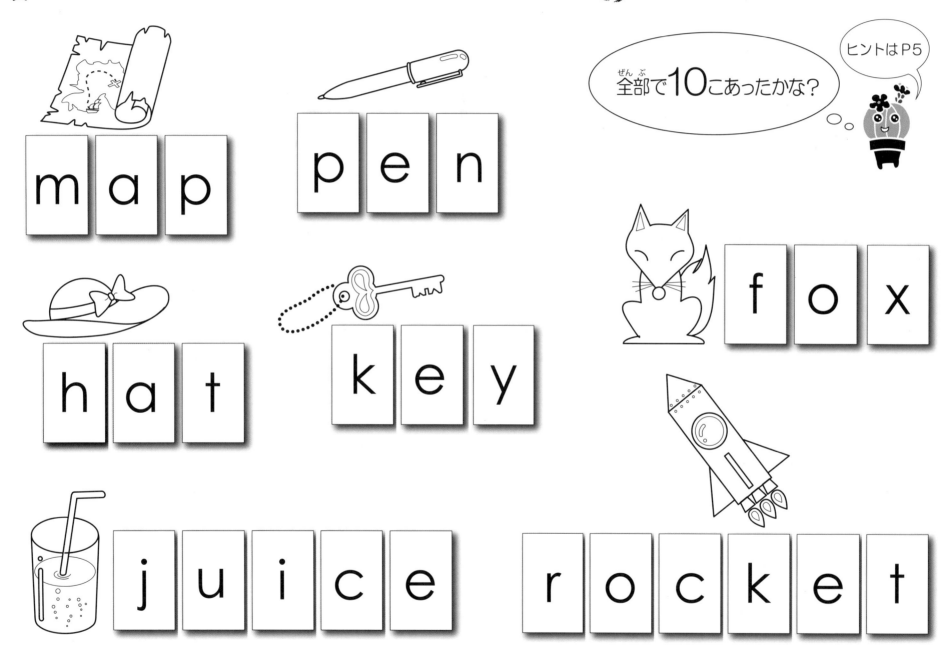

全部_{ぜんぶ}で10こあったかな？

ヒントはP5

map

pen

hat

key

fox

juice

rocket

Circle the vowels below. （お母さん文字（母音）を見つけて全部 ◯ をつけよう！）

全部で**10**こあったかな？ ヒントはP5

t o m a t o

f i r e

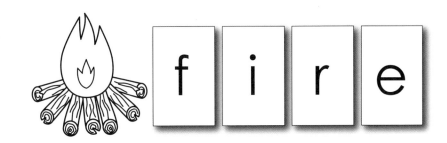

n u r s e

p e n g u i n

Write the missing letter on the line for each sentence.
（小文字を1字入れて文を完成させよう！）

言葉の前につく『a』と『an』。
いったい何がちがうかな？
答えはP14

① What is it?      It is an __nt.

② What is it?   It is a __emon.

③ What is it?      It is a __at.

④ What is it?      It is an __gg.

Write the missing letter on the line for each sentence.

（小文字を1字入れて文を完成させよう！）

言葉の前につく『a』と『an』。
いったい何がちがうかな？
答えはP14

① What is it?  It is a __rog.

② What is it?  It is a __ouse.

③ What is it?  It is a __trawberry.

④ What is it?  It is an __ctopus.

Write the missing letter on the line for each sentence.

（小文字を1字入れて文を完成させよう！）

言葉の前につく『a』と『an』。
いったい何がちがうかな？
答えはP14

①

What is it? It is a ___all.

②

What is it? It is **an** ___pron.

③

What is it? It is a ___o-yo.

④

What is it? It is a ___ree.

Write the missing letter on the line for each sentence.
（小文字を1字入れて文を完成させよう！）

言葉の前につく『a』と『an』。
いったい何がちがうかな？
答えはP14

① What is it?   It is a ___ow.

② What is it?   It is a ___ebra.

③ What is it?   It is a ___ueen.

④ What is it?   It is an ___mbrella.

-11-

Write the missing letter on the line for each sentence.
（小文字を1字入れて文を完成させよう！）

言葉の前につく『a』と『an』。
いったい何がちがうかな？
答えはP14

① What is it?    It is a __ig.

② What is it?   It is a __abbit.

③ What is it?   It is an __nion.

④ What is it?   It is a __atch.

Write the missing letter on the line for each sentence.

（小文字を1字入れて文を完成させよう！）

言葉の前につく『a』と『an』。いったい何がちがうかな？

答えはP14

① What is it?   It is a __orilla.

② What is it?   It is an __ron.

③ What is it?   It is a __iolin.

④ What is it?   It is a bo__.

『a』と『an』も「1つ」という同じ意味^{おな}だけど

使^{つか}われる時^{とき}が違^{ちが}うんだよ！

後^{うし}ろの言葉^{ことば}が**おかあさん文字^{もじ}の音^{おと}**で始^{はじ}まる時^{とき}は『an』

後^{うし}ろの言葉^{ことば}が**おかあさん文字以外^{もじいがい}の音^{おと}**で始^{はじ}まる時^{とき}は『a』

では、下^{した}の問題^{もんだい}で確^{たし}かめてみよう！

Read the sentences. （下^{した}の文^{ぶん}を読^よんでみよう!）

① It is a cake. 　　　　（それは1コのケーキです）

② It is an orange. 　　　（それは1コのオレンジです。）

③ It is a lion. 　　　　（それは1頭^{とう}のライオンです。）

④ It is an umbrella. 　（それは1本^{ぽん}のかさです。）

⑤ It is a book. 　　　（それは1さつの本^{ほん}です。）

Circle "a" or "an." (『a』か『an』を選んで ◯ をつけよう！)

＿の上の文字と音に
注意してね！

① 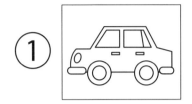 It is (a / an) <u>c</u>ar.

②  It is (a / an) <u>e</u>lephant.

③ 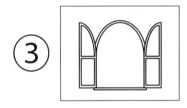 It is (a / an) <u>w</u>indow.

④ 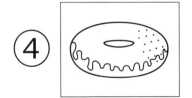 It is (a / an) <u>d</u>oughnut.

⑤  It is (a / an) <u>o</u>wl.

 Circle "a" or "an." (『a』か『an』を選んで ◯ をつけよう！)

 ＿ の上の文字と音に 注意してね！

① 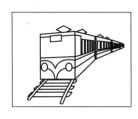 It is (a / an) _train.

②  It is (a / an) _iguana.

③  It is (a / an) _book.

④  It is (a / an) _kangaroo.

 音に注意！
⑤  It is (a / an) _uniform.

 文字は "u" だけど "y" の音で始まるよ！

Write "a" or "an" on the lines for each sentence. (『a』か『an』のどちらかを線の上に書こう！)

① 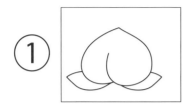 It is ___a___ peach.

②  It is _____ apple.

③  It is _____ eggplant.

④  It is _____ lion.

⑤ 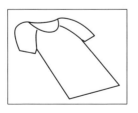 It is _____ undershirt.

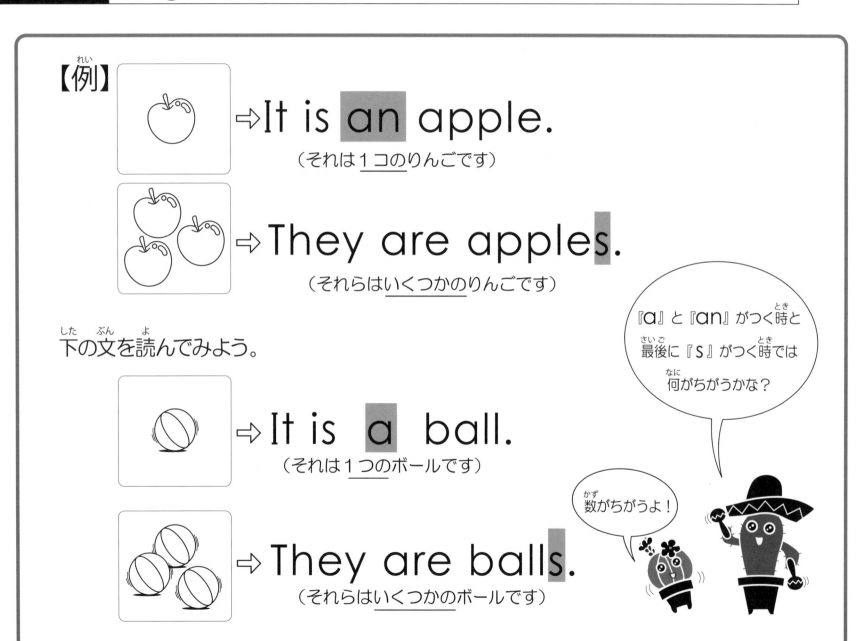

【例】

⇒It is an apple.
（それは1コのりんごです）

⇒They are apples.
（それらはいくつかのりんごです）

下の文を読んでみよう。

⇒It is a ball.
（それは1つのボールです）

⇒They are balls.
（それらはいくつかのボールです）

『a』と『an』がつく時と
最後に『s』がつく時では
何がちがうかな？

数がちがうよ！

What is missing? Fill in the blanks. (__ に当てはまる文字は何かな?)

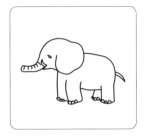 ⇒ It is ___ elephant.

（それは1とうのぞうです）

『a / an /s 』のどれかを入れてね！

 ⇒ They are elephant_.

（それらはなんとうかのぞうです）

 ⇒ It is __ violin.

（それは1つのヴァイオリンです）

 ⇒ They are violin_.

（それらはいくつかのヴァイオリンです）

Match the sentences to the correct pictures.

（文に合った絵を選んで線で結ぼう！）

① They are <u>kite</u>s. •

② It is <u>a horse</u>. •

③ They are <u>flowers</u>. •

④ It is <u>an igloo</u>. •

Match the sentences to the correct pictures.
（文に合った絵を選んで線で結ぼう！）

① They are <u>dog**s**</u>. •

② They are <u>egg**s**</u>. •

③ It is <u>**an** ant</u>. •

④ It is <u>**a** star</u>. •

Say it! Match the sentences to the correct pictures.
（文に合った絵を選んで線で結ぼう！）

① It is a chair. •

② They are crabs. •

③ They are watermelons. •

④ It is an ambulance. •

①

A: It is a sock.

B: They are socks.

▢

②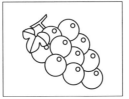

A: It is a grape.

B: They are grapes.

▢

③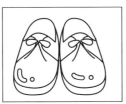

A: It is a shoe.

B: They are shoes.

▢

④

A: It is a glove.

B: They are gloves.

▢

Read the sentences. (下の文を読んでみよう!) （ひとりの人/ひとつのもの）

わたし

I am a boy.

あなた

You are a boy.

かれ

He is a boy.

かのじょ

She is a girl.

それ

It is a tree.

（ふたりより多い人/ふたつより多いもの）

we わたしたち

We are boys.

you あなたたち

You are girls.

they かれら（かのじょたち）それら

They are friends.

いっぱい あるけど できるかな？

Read the sentences. (下の文を読んでみよう！)

① I am a boy. （ぼくは男の子です。）

② You are a boy. （あなたは男の子です。）

③ He is a boy. （かれは男の子です。）

④ She is a girl. （かのじょは女の子です。）

⑤ It is a cat. （それはねこです。）

⑥ We are girls. （わたしたちは女の子です。）

⑦ You are boys. （あなたたちは男の子です。）

⑧ They are boys. （かれらは男の子です。）

Write the words three times each on the dotted lines.
（線の上に「am」「is」「are」を書いてみよう！3回くらい書けるかな？）

I am

He is

She is

It is

You are

We are

They are

『なかよしのことば』は覚えたかな？

-27-

Circle "am," "is" or "are." (『am』か『is』か『are』を選んで〇をつけよう！)

①  I $\left(\begin{array}{c} \text{am} \\ \text{is} \\ \text{are} \end{array}\right)$ a boy.

② 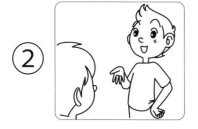 You $\left(\begin{array}{c} \text{am} \\ \text{is} \\ \text{are} \end{array}\right)$ a boy.

③  She $\left(\begin{array}{c} \text{am} \\ \text{is} \\ \text{are} \end{array}\right)$ a girl.

④  He $\left(\begin{array}{c} \text{am} \\ \text{is} \\ \text{are} \end{array}\right)$ a boy.

① 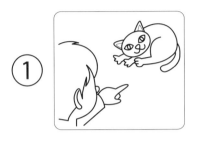 It $\left(\begin{array}{c} \text{am} \\ \text{is} \\ \text{are} \end{array}\right)$ a cat.

② You $\left(\begin{array}{c} \text{am} \\ \text{is} \\ \text{are} \end{array}\right)$ a girl.

③ We $\left(\begin{array}{c} \text{am} \\ \text{is} \\ \text{are} \end{array}\right)$ boys.

④  They $\left(\begin{array}{c} \text{am} \\ \text{is} \\ \text{are} \end{array}\right)$ girls.

Circle "am," "is" or "are." （『am』か『is』か『are』を選んで〇をつけよう！）

①  <u>We</u> $\begin{pmatrix} \text{am} \\ \text{is} \\ \text{are} \end{pmatrix}$ friends.

② She $\begin{pmatrix} \text{am} \\ \text{is} \\ \text{are} \end{pmatrix}$ a nurse.

③  <u>It</u> $\begin{pmatrix} \text{am} \\ \text{is} \\ \text{are} \end{pmatrix}$ a tree.

④ <u>You</u> $\begin{pmatrix} \text{am} \\ \text{is} \\ \text{are} \end{pmatrix}$ students.

Circle "am," "is" or "are." （『am』か『is』か『are』を選んで ◯ をつけよう！）

① 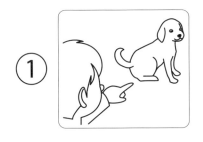 <u>It</u> $\begin{pmatrix} \text{am} \\ \text{is} \\ \text{are} \end{pmatrix}$ a dog.

②  <u>You</u> $\begin{pmatrix} \text{am} \\ \text{is} \\ \text{are} \end{pmatrix}$ a teacher.

③  <u>He</u> $\begin{pmatrix} \text{am} \\ \text{is} \\ \text{are} \end{pmatrix}$ a firefighter.

④  <u>They</u> $\begin{pmatrix} \text{am} \\ \text{is} \\ \text{are} \end{pmatrix}$ brothers.

Trace the words and circle "am," "is" or "are" to make a correct sentence.

（点線の文字をなぞった後『am』か『is』か『are』を選んで◯をつけよう！）

① It (am is are) a panda.

② We (am is are) students.

③ You (am is are) pilots.

④ They (am is are) dentists.

Trace the words and circle "am," "is" or "are" to make a correct sentence.

（点線の文字をなぞった後『am』か『is』か『are』を選んで◯をつけよう！）

① I $\left(\begin{array}{c} am \\ is \\ are \end{array}\right)$ a doctor.

② You $\left(\begin{array}{c} am \\ is \\ are \end{array}\right)$ a cook.

③ He $\left(\begin{array}{c} am \\ is \\ are \end{array}\right)$ a teacher.

④ She $\left(\begin{array}{c} am \\ is \\ are \end{array}\right)$ a vet.

Write "am," "is" or "are" on the lines for each sentence.
（『am』か『is』か『are』を線の上に書こう！）

① It _____is_____ a panda.

② We _____ students.

③ You _____ pilots.

④ They _____ dentists.

Write "am," "is" or "are" on the lines for each sentence.
（『am』か『is』か『are』を線の上に書こう！）

① I _____ a doctor.

② You _____ a cook.

③ He _____ a teacher.

④ She _____ a vet.

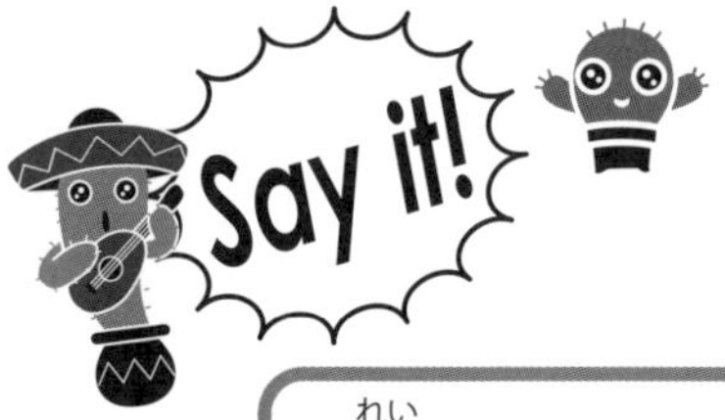

【例】

What are you?
（あなたはなあに？）

Welcome to our costume party!
わたしたちのコスチュームパーティーにようこそ！
いろいろなものに変装しちゃうよ！

I am a nurse.
（わたしはかんごしです。）

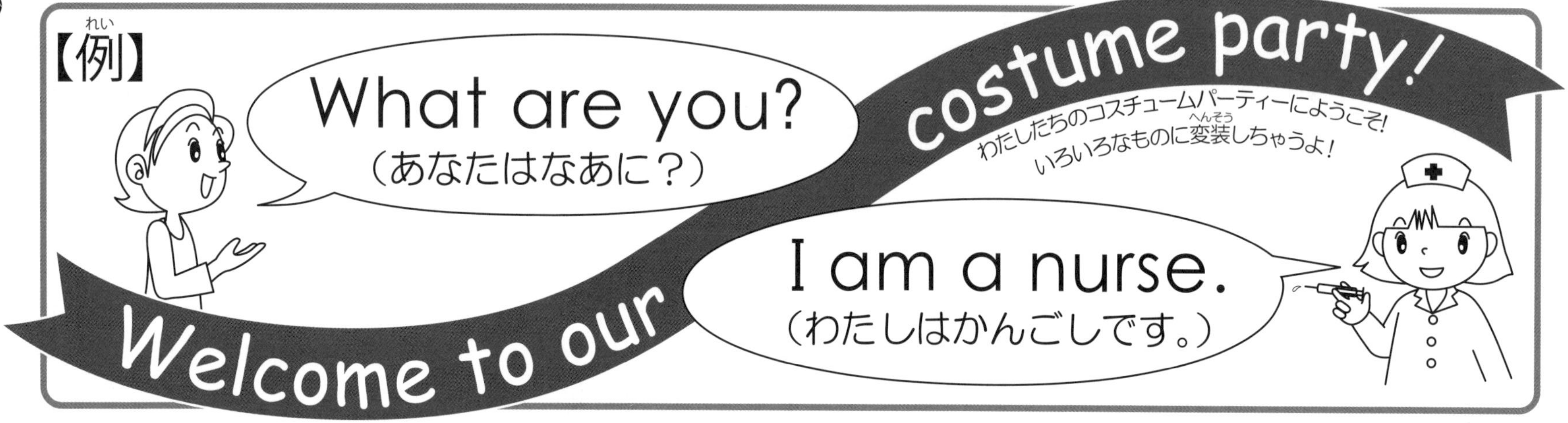

① What are you?

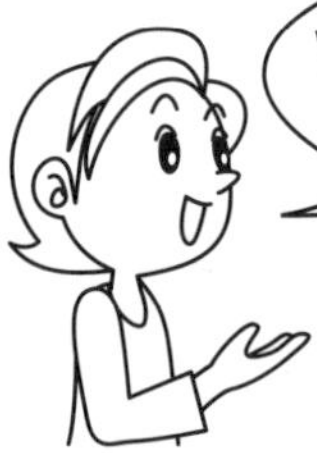

I ＿＿＿＿＿ a doctor.

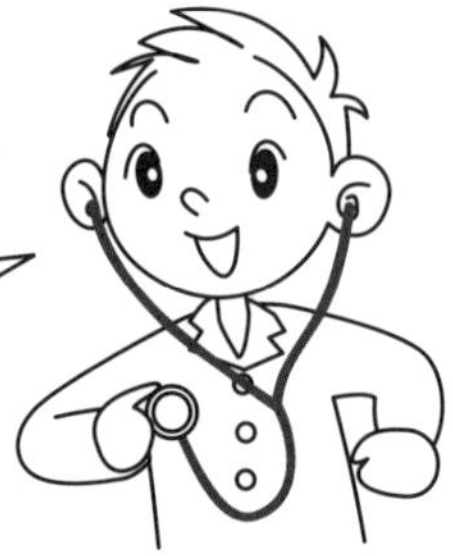

② What are you?

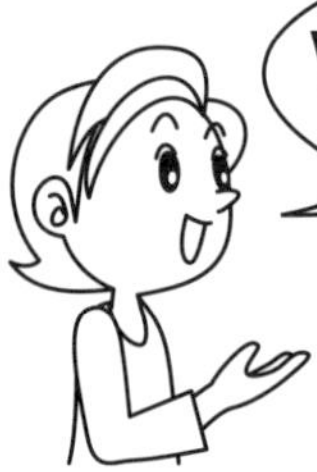

I ＿＿＿＿＿ a pilot.

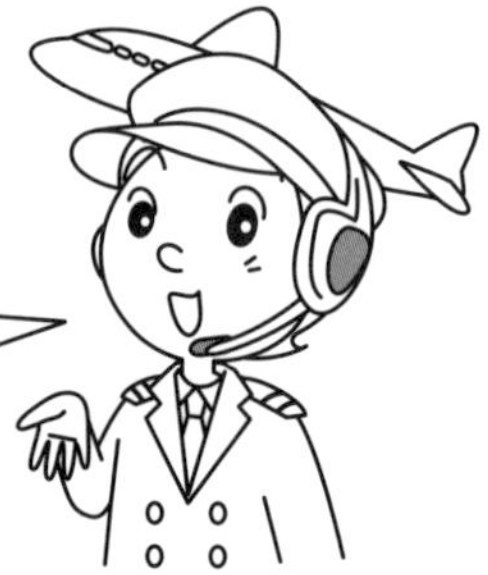

Write the correct word on the lines and read the sentence.

(<u>_____</u> に正しい英語を入れよう！ その後で文を読んでみよう！)

1 What is he?

He _____ a zookeeper.

2 What is she?

She _____ a princess.

3 What are you?

We _____ bakers.

4 What is it?

It _____ a jellyfish.

スペシャル問題！！

Special question!

Write the correct word on the lines and read the sentence.
（＿＿＿ に正しい英語を入れよう！ その後で文を読んでみよう！）

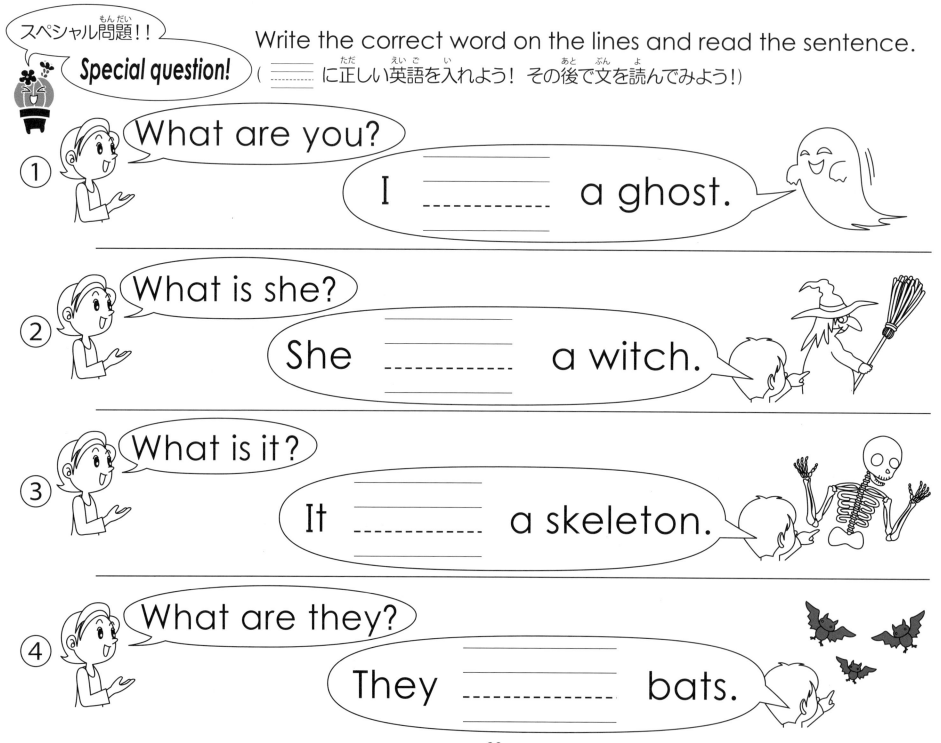

① What are you?

I ＿＿＿＿＿ a ghost.

② What is she?

She ＿＿＿＿＿ a witch.

③ What is it?

It ＿＿＿＿＿ a skeleton.

④ What are they?

They ＿＿＿＿＿ bats.

Write the correct word on the lines and read the sentence.
(===== に正しい英語を入れよう！ その後で文を読んでみよう！)
ただ えいご い　　　　　　あと ぶん よ

① What is he?

He _____ a king.

② What is she?

She _____ a teacher.

③ What are you?

We _____ students.

④ What are they?

They _____ firefighters.

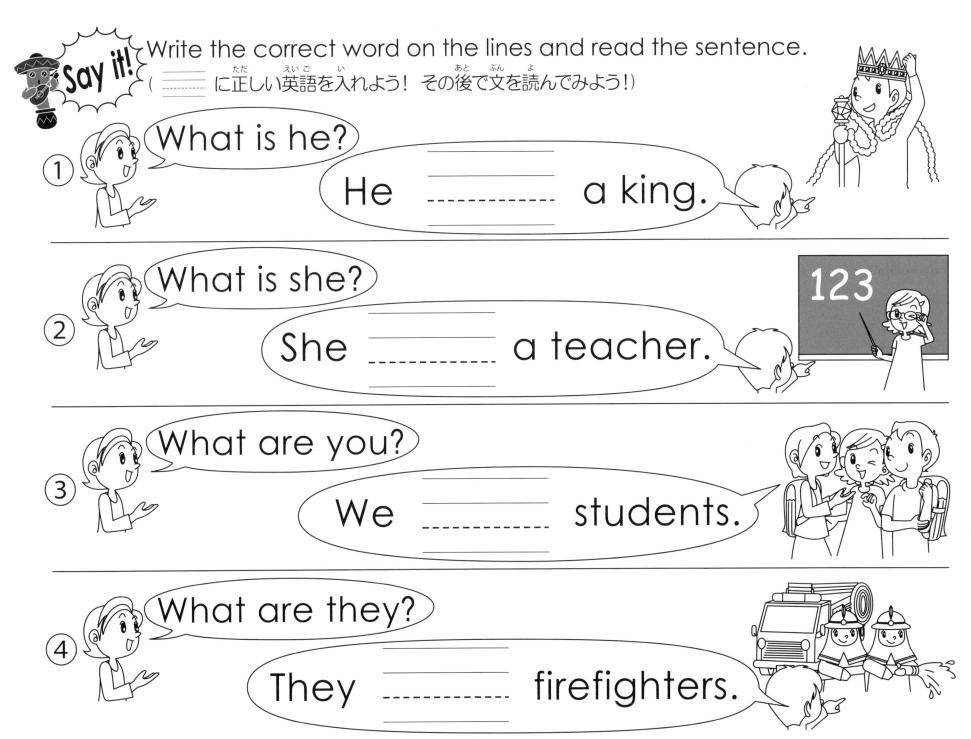

 Trace the words and read the sentences. (点線の英語をなぞってから文を読んでみよう!)

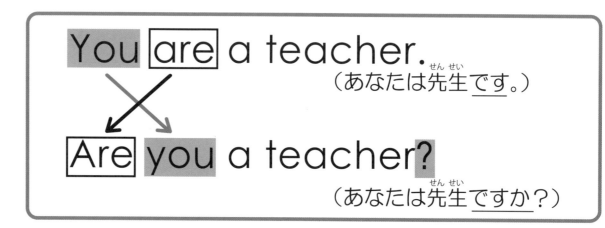

You are a teacher.
（あなたは先生です。）

Are you a teacher?
（あなたは先生ですか？）

あなたは先生です。 ⇒ You are a teacher.

あなたは先生ですか？ ⇒ Are you a teacher?

文のはじめの文字は
大文字になるよ！
しつもんのときは
"?" も
忘れないでね！

Trace the words and read the sentences. (点線の英語をなぞってから文を読んでみよう!)

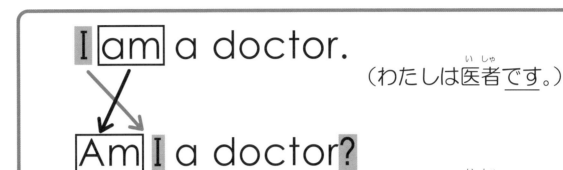

I am a doctor.
（わたしは医者です。）

Am I a doctor?
（わたしは医者ですか？）

とくべつ 「わたし」の意味の "I" はいつも大文字だよ!

わたしは医者です。 ⇒ I am a doctor.

わたしは医者ですか？ ⇒ Am I a doctor?

文のはじめの文字は大文字になるよ! しつもんのときは "?" も忘れないでね!

Trace the words and read the sentences. （点線の英語をなぞってから文を読んでみよう！）

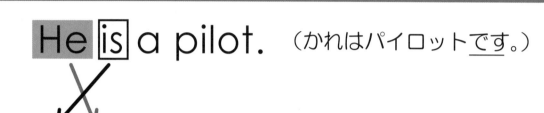

He is a pilot. （かれはパイロット<u>です</u>。）

Is he a pilot? （かれはパイロット<u>ですか</u>？）

かれはパイロットです。　⇒  He is a pilot.

かれはパイロットですか？　⇒ Is he a pilot?

文のはじめの文字は
大文字になるよ！

しつもんのときは
"？" も

忘れないでね！

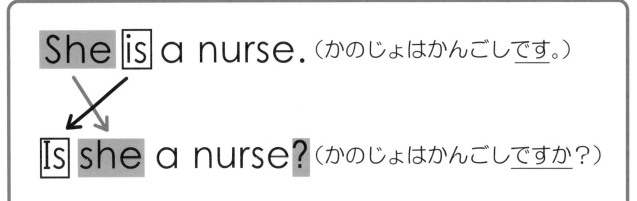

She is a nurse.（かのじょはかんごしです。）

Is she a nurse?（かのじょはかんごしですか？）

かのじょはかんごしです。　⇨　 a nurse.

かのじょはかんごしですか？⇨　 a nurse?

文のはじめの文字は
大文字になるよ！

しつもんのときは
"?" も
忘れないでね！

-43-

It is a dog. （それは犬です。）

Is it a dog? （それは犬ですか？）

それは犬です。 ⇒ 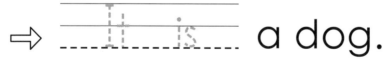 a dog.

それは犬ですか？ ⇒  a dog?

文のはじめの文字は
大文字になるよ！
しつもんのときは
"?" も
忘れないでね！

Trace the words and read the sentences. (点線の英語をなぞってから文を読んでみよう！)

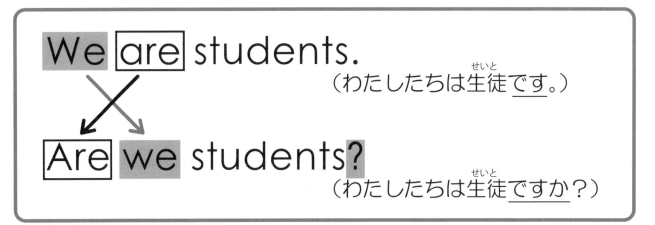

We are students.
（わたしたちは生徒です。）

Are we students?
（わたしたちは生徒ですか？）

わたしたちは生徒です。　⇒　We are students.

わたしたちは生徒ですか？　⇒　Are we students?

文のはじめの文字は
大文字になるよ！
しつもんのときは
"?" も
忘れないでね！

Trace the words and read the sentences. (点線の英語をなぞってから文を読んでみよう!)

You are dancers.
（あなたたちはダンサーです。）

Are you dancers?
（あなたたちはダンサーですか？）

あなたたちは
ダンサーです。 ⇒ You are dancers.

あなたたちは
ダンサーですか？ ⇒ Are you dancers?

文のはじめの文字は
大文字になるよ！

しつもんのときは
"?" も
忘れないでね！

They are firefighters.
（かれらは消防士<u>です</u>。）

Are they firefighters?
（かれらは消防士<u>ですか？</u>）

かれらは
消防士です。 ⇒ 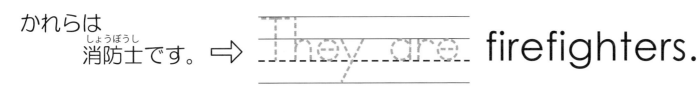 firefighters.

かれらは
消防士ですか？ ⇒  firefighters?

文のはじめの文字は
大文字になるよ！
しつもんのときは
"?" も
忘れないでね！

Write the missing words on the lines. (‑‑‑‑‑ に英語を書いて文を完成させよう！)

とくべつ

「わたし」の意味の "I" はいつも大文字だよ！

① I am a doctor.　　　　　　　　(わたしは医者です。)

⇒ ＿＿＿＿ ＿＿＿＿ a doctor? (わたしは医者ですか？)

② You are a cook.　　　　　　(あなたはコックです。)

⇒ ＿＿＿＿ ＿＿＿＿ a cook?　(あなたはコックですか？)

③ He is a pilot.　　　　　　　(かれはパイロットです。)

⇒ ＿＿＿＿ ＿＿＿＿ a pilot?　(かれはパイロットですか？)

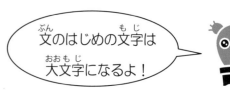

文のはじめの文字は大文字になるよ！

 Write the missing words on the lines. (＿＿ に英語を書いて文を完成させよう！)

① She is a nurse. （かのじょはかんごしです。）

⇒ ＿＿＿＿ ＿＿＿＿ a nurse? （かのじょはかんごしですか？）

② It is a dog. （それは犬です。）

⇒ ＿＿＿＿ ＿＿＿＿ a dog? （それは犬ですか？）

③ We are students. （わたしたちは生徒です。）

⇒ ＿＿＿＿ ＿＿＿＿ students? （わたしたちは生徒ですか？）

しつもんのとき、1番目と2番目が入れかわるんだよね！

Write the missing words on the lines. (＿＿＿ に英語を書いて文を完成させよう!)

① You are dancers.　　　　　（あなたたちはダンサーです。）

⇒ ＿＿＿＿＿ ＿＿＿＿＿ dancers? （あなたたちはダンサーですか？）

② They are firefighters.　　　　（かれらは消防士です。）

⇒ ＿＿＿＿＿ ＿＿＿＿＿ firefighters? （かれらは消防士ですか？）

しつもんのとき、
どこが入れかわるのか
覚えたかな？

Circle the correct word and read the sentence. （正しい英語に ◯ をつけ文を読んでみよう！）

① (Are / Am) <u>I</u> a queen?

② (Are / Am) <u>you</u> a doctor?

③ (Are / Is) <u>she</u> a nurse?

④ (Is / Are) <u>he</u> a teacher?

⑤ (Are / Am) <u>they</u> firefighters?

Circle the correct word and read the sentence. (正しい英語に◯をつけ文を読んでみよう！)

① (Is / Am) <u>he</u> a cook?

② (Are / Am) <u>they</u> tigers?

③ (Are / Is) <u>we</u> dancers?

④ (Is / Are) <u>it</u> a rabbit?

⑤ (Are / Am) <u>I</u> a girl?

Circle the correct word and read the sentence. (正しい英語に ◯ をつけ文を読んでみよう！)

① (You are / Are you) a baker?

② (He is / Is he) a police officer.

③ (You are / Are you) singers?

④ (It is / Is it) a pumpkin.

⑤ (We are / Are we) scientists?

文のさいごが "?" のときと "." で終わるときでは 大きく違うんだよ！ 気をつけてね！

① (I am / Am I) a waitress.

② (She is / Is she) a zookeeper?

③ (You are / Are you) pilots?

④ (It is / Is it) an alligator.

⑤ (They are / Are they) pancakes?

① (I am / Am I) a farmer.

② (She is / Is she) a pianist?

③ (You are / Are you) a king?

④ (He is / Is he) a soccer player.

⑤ (They are / Are they) giraffes?

Section 7　Questions and Answers （こたえの文のつくり方）

【例1】

Is it a cat?

Yes, it <u>is</u>. （はい、そうです。）

No, it <u>is</u> **not**. （いいえ、ちがいます。）
（長い形）

No, it <u>isn't</u>. （いいえ、ちがいます。）
（短い形）

※ **,** マークは英語のことばを短くしてくれるよ。

 Read the sentences. （文を読んでみよう！）

人と話すときは「短い形」の方を使うよ！使えるようにしてね！

No, you are **not**. ⇨**No**, you **aren't**.

No, we are **not**. ⇨**No**, we **aren't**.

No, they are **not**. ⇨**No**, they **aren't**.

No, he is **not**. ⇨**No**, he **isn't**.

No, she is **not**. ⇨**No**, she **isn't**.

No, it is **not**. ⇨**No**, it **isn't**.

【例2】 Are you a teacher?

「短い形」になる場所が上の文とはちがうよ！

スペシャルケース

Yes, I <u>am</u>. （はい、そうです。）

No, <u>I am</u> **not**. （いいえ、ちがいます。）

No, <u>I'm</u> **not**. （いいえ、ちがいます。）

 Match the correct forms. （左の文にあう「短い形」と線でむすぼう！）

①No, you are not. •　　　• No, they aren't.

②No, we are not. •　　　• No, you aren't.

③No, they are not. •　　　• No, it isn't.

④No, he is not. •　　　• No, we aren't.

⑤No, she is not. •　　　• No, she isn't.

⑥No, it is not. •　　　• No, he isn't.

 Trace the sentences and read it.（次の点線の文をなぞってから読んでみよう！）

 スペシャルケース

No, I am **not**. ⇨  No, I'm not.

 Read the sentences. （文を読んでみよう！）

①  Am I a prince?　Yes, I <u>am</u>.

② Am I a prince?　No, I<u>'m not</u>.

③  Am I a police officer?　Yes, you <u>are</u>.

④ Am I a police officer?　No, you <u>aren't</u>.

⑤ Are you a scientist?　Yes, I <u>am</u>.

⑥  Are you a scientist?　No, I<u>'m not</u>.

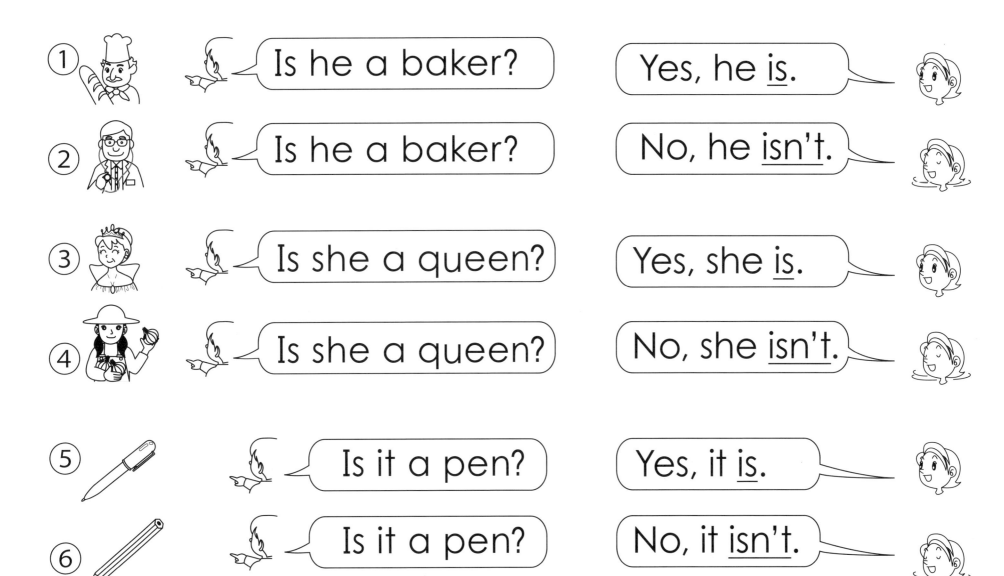

① Is he a baker? — Yes, he <u>is</u>.

② Is he a baker? — No, he <u>isn't</u>.

③ Is she a queen? — Yes, she <u>is</u>.

④ Is she a queen? — No, she <u>isn't</u>.

⑤ Is it a pen? — Yes, it <u>is</u>.

⑥ Is it a pen? — No, it <u>isn't</u>.

 Read the sentences. (文を読んでみよう!)

①  Are we firefighters?　Yes, you <u>are</u>.

② Are we firefighters?　No, you <u>aren't</u>.

③ Are you students?　Yes, we <u>are</u>.

④ Are you students?　No, we <u>aren't</u>.

⑤  Are they pigs?　Yes, they <u>are</u>.

⑥ Are they pigs?　No, they <u>aren't</u>.

-60-

Choose the correct answer. （正しい答えを選んで ◯ をつけよう!）

① Are you a pilot?

A : Yes, I <u>am</u>.

B : No, I<u>'m not</u>.

☐
☐

② Is it a ladybug?

A : Yes, it <u>is</u>.

B : No, it <u>isn't</u>.

☐
☐

③ Am I a pianist?

A : Yes, you <u>are</u>.

B : No, you <u>aren't</u>.

☐
☐

 Choose the correct answer. （正しい答えを選んで◯をつけよう！）

① Is she a waitress?

A：Yes, she <u>is</u>.

B：No, she <u>isn't</u>.

② Are you soccer players?

A：Yes, we <u>are</u>.

B：No, we <u>aren't</u>.

③ Is he a dentist?

A：Yes, he <u>is</u>.

B：No, he <u>isn't</u>.

④ Is she a cook?

A：Yes, she <u>is</u>.

B：No, she <u>isn't</u>.

Choose the correct answer. （<ruby>正<rt>ただ</rt></ruby>しい<ruby>答<rt>こた</rt></ruby>えを<ruby>選<rt>えら</rt></ruby>んで ◯ をつけよう！）

① Are we pilots?

A：Yes, you <u>are</u>.

B：No, you <u>aren't</u>.

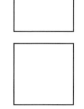

② Is it a mouse?

A：Yes, it <u>is</u>.

B：No, it <u>isn't</u>.

③ Are they farmers?

A：Yes, they <u>are</u>.

B：No, they <u>aren't</u>.

Write the correct word on the lines to complete the questions, and trace the words in the answers. (＿＿の上に正しい英語を入れて質問文を完成させよう！答えの文の言葉をなぞろう！)

① ＿＿＿＿ he a police officer?

Yes, he __is__.

② ＿＿＿＿ you a scientist?

No, I __'m not__.

③ ＿＿＿＿ she a pianist?

No, she __isn't__.

④ ＿＿＿＿ it a riceball?

Yes, it __is__.

⑤ ＿＿＿＿ they bakers?

Yes, they __are__.

-64-

Write the correct word on the lines to complete the questions, and trace the words in the answers. (_____の上に正しい英語を入れて質問文を完成させよう！答えの文の言葉をなぞろう！)

1. _____ we dancers?

   Yes, you _are_.

2. _____ I a fisherman?

   No, you _aren't_.

3. _____ you office workers?

   Yes, we _are_.

4. _____ it a grasshopper?

   No, it _isn't_.

5. _____ she a waitress?

   Yes, she _is_.

Grammar 1で出てきたよ！
覚えてるかな？

Trace the verbs below. Then match the sentences to the correct pictures. (次の点線のことばをなぞってから、あてはまる絵と線でむすぼう！)

① I go to school. •

•

② I close the curtains. •

•

③ I sit down. •

•

④ I stand up. •

•

⑤ I open a box. •

•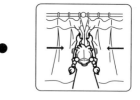

⑥ I swim in a pool. •

•

Choose the correct verb from the ▭ and write it on the line for each sentence.

（▭ から正しい英語を選んで _____ に書こう！）

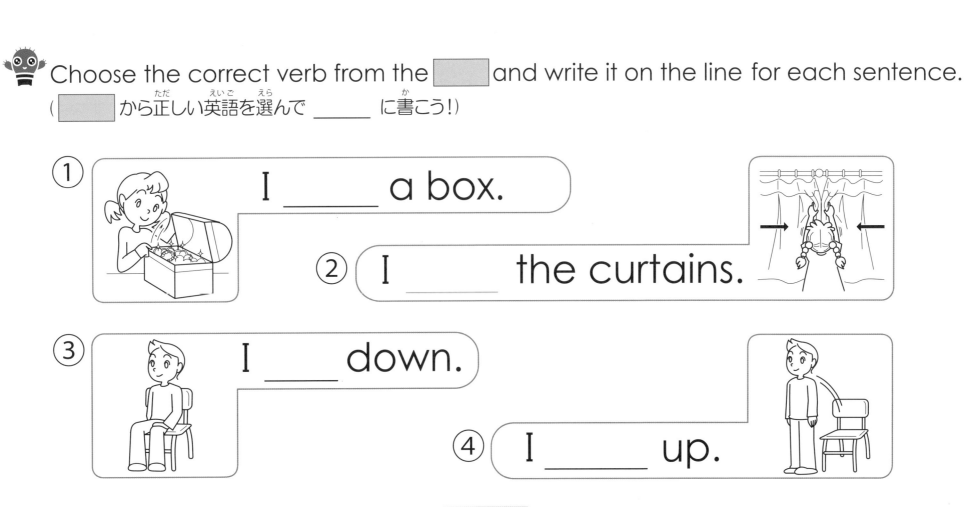

① I _____ a box.

② I _____ the curtains.

③ I _____ down.

④ I _____ up.

⑤ I _____ to school.

⑥ I _____ in a pool .

go　　open　　stand　　sit　　swim　　close

Trace the verbs below. Then match the sentences to the correct pictures. (次の点線のことばをなぞってから、あてはまる絵と線でむすぼう！)

① I pull a rope. •

② I run in the park. •

③ I push a button. •

④ I throw a ball. •

⑤ I walk to school. •

⑥ I catch a ball. •

Choose the correct verb from the ▢ and write it on the line for each sentence.

(▢ から正しい英語を選んで _____ に書こう！)

①  I _____ to school.

② I _____ in the park.

③  I _____ a ball.

④ I _____ a ball.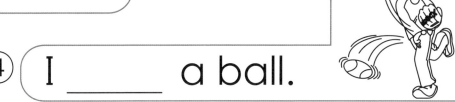

⑤  I _____ a rope.

⑥ I _____ a button.

| run | walk | catch | throw | pull | push |

Trace the verbs below. Then match the sentences to the correct pictures. (次の点線のことばをなぞってから、あてはまる絵と線でむすぼう!)

Grammar 1 で出てきたよ！
覚えてるかな？

① I cut paper. •

② I eat curry. •

③ I sing in the room. •

④ I cook pancakes. •

⑤ I drink water. •

⑥ I sleep in my bed. •

① I ＿＿＿＿ pancakes.

② I ＿＿＿ water.

③ I ＿＿＿＿ in my bed.

④ I ＿＿＿ curry.

⑤ I ＿＿＿ paper.

⑥ I ＿＿＿ in the room.

drink   cook   cut   sing   eat   sleep

 Read the sentences. (文を読んでみよう！)

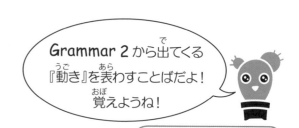

① I wash my hands.

② I have a balloon.

③ I look at a picture.

④ I like dolls.

⑤ I play the piano.

⑥ I study English.

Trace the verbs below. Then match the sentences to the correct pictures.
（次の点線のことばをなぞってから、あてはまる絵と線でむすぼう！）

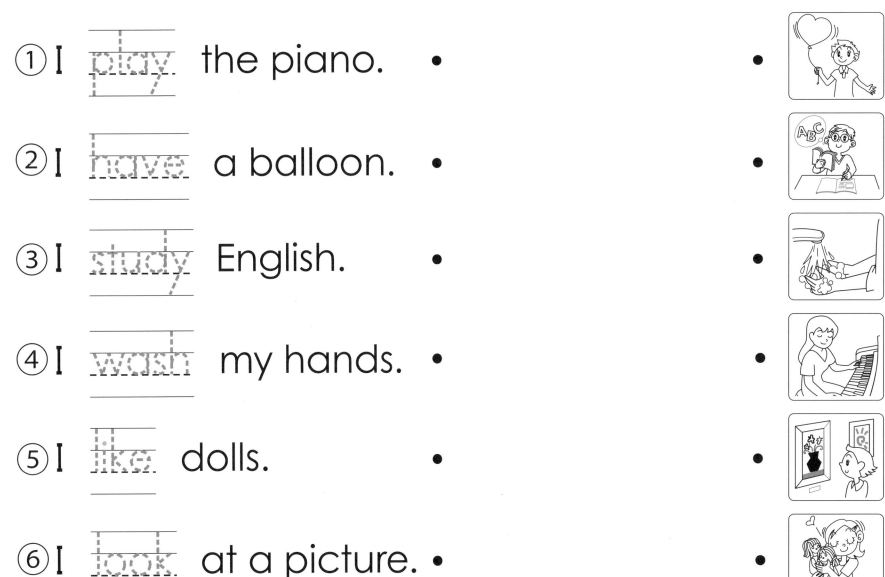

① I play the piano. •

② I have a balloon. •

③ I study English. •

④ I wash my hands. •

⑤ I like dolls. •

⑥ I look at a picture. •

Read the sentences. （文を読んでみよう！）

Grammar 2 から出てくる『動き』を表わすことばだよ！覚えようね！

①  I <u>fly</u> in an airplane.

② I <u>listen</u> to music.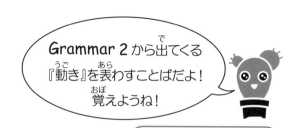

③  I <u>climb</u> a ladder.

④ I <u>jump</u> on the bed.

⑤  I <u>draw</u> a picture.

⑥ I <u>touch</u> the wall.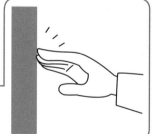

Trace the verbs below. Then match the sentences to the correct pictures.
（次の点線のことばをなぞってから、あてはまる絵と線でむすぼう！）

① I jump on the bed. •

② I draw a picture. •

③ I touch the wall. •

④ I fly in an airplane. •

⑤ I climb a ladder. •

⑥ I listen to music. •

 Read the sentences. (文を読んでみよう！)

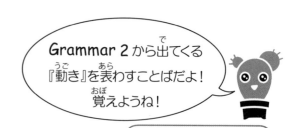 Grammar 2 から出てくる『動き』を表わすことばだよ！覚えようね！

① I read a book.

② I write a letter.

③ I ride a bike.

④ I make a necklace.

⑤ I put a bowl on the table.

⑥ I pick flowers.

Trace the verbs below. Then match the sentences to the correct pictures.
（次の点線のことばをなぞってから、あてはまる絵と線でむすぼう！）

① I write a letter. •

② I make a necklace. •

③ I put a bowl on the • table.

④ I ride a bike. •

⑤ I pick flowers. •

⑥ I read a book. •

①  I $\left(\begin{array}{c}\text{have}\\\text{sleep}\end{array}\right)$ a balloon.

②  I $\left(\begin{array}{c}\text{eat}\\\text{fly}\end{array}\right)$ in an airplane.

③ 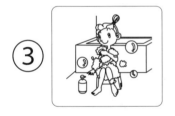 I $\left(\begin{array}{c}\text{drink}\\\text{wash}\end{array}\right)$ my body.

④  I $\left(\begin{array}{c}\text{cook}\\\text{like}\end{array}\right)$ dolls.

⑤  I $\left(\begin{array}{c}\text{close}\\\text{jump}\end{array}\right)$ on the bed.

どっちのことばが 絵に合うか わかるかな?

①  I (look / throw) at a picture.

②  I (open / climb) a ladder.

③  I (draw / pull) a picture.

④ 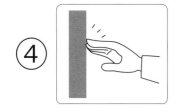 I (touch / walk) the wall.

⑤  I (make / cut) a necklace.

どっちのことばが
絵に合うか
わかるかな?

 Circle the correct verb and read the sentence. (正しい英語に〇をつけ文を読んでみよう!)

①  I (push / play) soccer.

②  I (sing / listen) to music.

③  I (study / stand) English.

 どっちのことばが 絵に合うか わかるかな?

④  I (put / sit) a bowl on the table.

 Circle the correct verb and read the sentence. (正しい英語に◯をつけ文を読んでみよう!)

 ① I (catch / pick) flowers.

 ② I (read / swim) a book.

 ③ I (close / write) a letter.

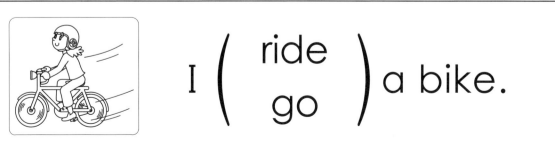 ④ I (ride / go) a bike.

 どっちのことばが
絵に合うか
わかるかな?

Choose the correct word from the ▢ and write it on the lines.
(▢ から正しい英語を選んで ═══ に書こう！)

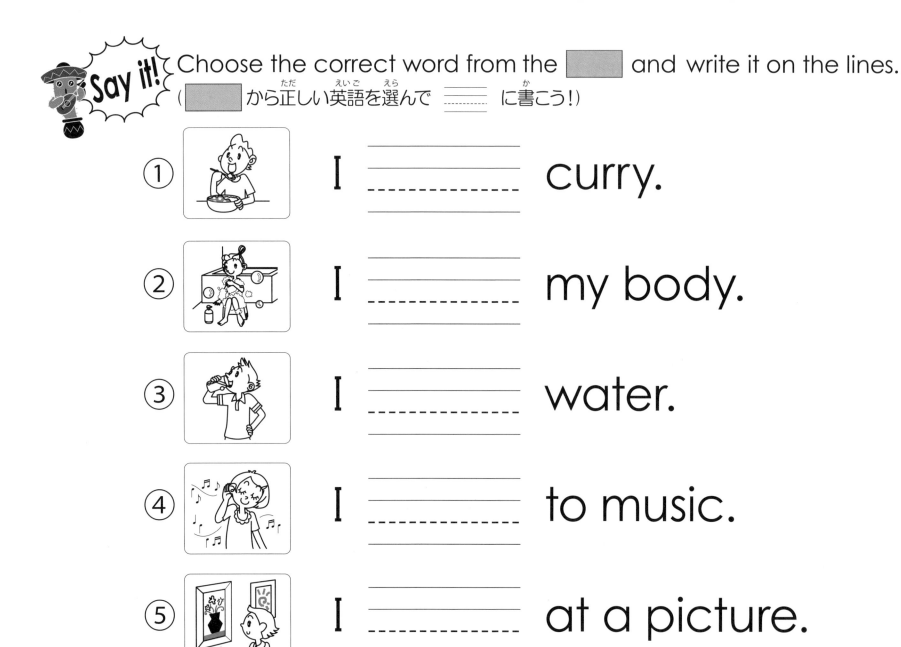

① I _____ curry.

② I _____ my body.

③ I _____ water.

④ I _____ to music.

⑤ I _____ at a picture.

wash   look   listen   eat   drink

Say it! Choose the correct word from the  and write it on the lines.
（　　　から正しい英語を選んで ‐‐‐‐‐ に書こう！）

①  I ‐‐‐‐‐‐‐‐‐‐‐‐‐ a koala.

②  I ‐‐‐‐‐‐‐‐‐‐‐‐‐ in an airplane.

③  I ‐‐‐‐‐‐‐‐‐‐‐‐‐ soccer.

④  I ‐‐‐‐‐‐‐‐‐‐‐‐‐ a button.

⑤  I ‐‐‐‐‐‐‐‐‐‐‐‐‐ a cake.

| play | fly | touch | make | push |

Say it! Choose the correct word from the ▢ and write it on the lines.
(▢ から正しい英語を選んで ═══ に書こう！)

①  I _____ a basket.

②  I _____ in my bed.

③  I _____ a pancake.

④  I _____ math.

⑤  I _____ cats.

cook　　like　　have　　sleep　　study

Choose the correct word from the and write it on the lines.

(から正しい英語を選んでに書こう!)

① 　I _____ a letter.

② 　I _____ the curtains.

③ 　I _____ a book.

④ 　I _____ a ladder.

⑤　I _____ a train.

ride　　climb　　read　　write　　close

Section 5 と Section 8 で習ったことに『～ing』を組み合わせると『 今、 ～しています』という表現になるよ！

【例】

I am washing my hands. （わたしは 今、手をあらっ<u>ています</u>。）

He is playing soccer. （かれは 今、サッカーをし<u>ています</u>。）

They are jumping on the bed. （かれらは 今、ベッドの上で ジャンプし<u>ています</u>。）

Say it! Read the sentences. （文を読んでみよう！）

①  I am listening to music. （わたしは 今、音楽をきい<u>ています</u>。）

②  I am reading a book. （わたしは 今、本を読ん<u>でいます</u>。）

③  I am looking at a picture. （わたしは 今、絵を見<u>ています</u>。）

What are you doing?
（今、何してるの？）

I am walking.
（わたしは 今、歩いています。）

Trace the letters and read the sentences.
（点線の文字をなぞって「今〜している」文を読んでみよう！）

①  I am drinking milk. （わたしは 今、ミルクをのんでいます。）

②  I am playing the piano.
（わたしは 今、ピアノをひいています。）

③  I am picking strawberries.
（わたしは 今、いちごをつんでいます。）

④  I am eating curry. （わたしは 今、カレーを食べています。）

Trace the letters and read the sentences. (点線の文字をなぞって「今～している」文を読んでみよう！)

What are you doing?

（今、何してるの？）

① I am climbing a tree. （わたしは今、木にのぼっています。）

② I am washing my body. （わたしは今、体をあらっています。）

③ I am flying in an airplane.
（わたしは今、飛行機で飛んでいます。）

④ I am pushing a button.
（わたしは今、ボタンを押しています。）

Trace the letters. Then read the sentences and see how they are different.
（次の点線のことばをなぞってから、2つの文を読んでちがいを見つけよう！）

① You walk every day.（あなたは毎日あるきます。）

You are walking.　　（あなたは今、あるいています。）

② He plays soccer every day.

He is playing soccer.（彼は毎日サッカーをします。）

（彼は今、サッカーをしています。）

③ She cooks every day.（彼女は毎日料理をします。）

She is cooking.　　（彼女は今、料理をしています。）

④ It runs every day.（それは毎日走ります。）

It is running.　　（それは今、走っています。）

Trace the letters. Then read the sentences and see how they are different.
（次の点線のことばをなぞってから、2つの文を読んでちがいを見つけよう！）

① We draw pictures every day. （私たちは毎日絵をかきます。）

We are drawing pictures. （私たちは今、絵をかいています。）

② They wash the dishes every day.

（彼らは毎日お皿をあらいます。）

They are washing the dishes.

（彼らは今、お皿をあらっています。）

③ You study every day. （あなたたちは毎日べんきょうします。）

You are studying. （あなたたちは今、べんきょうしています。）

 Complete the sentences. (——— に合うことばを入れて文を完成させよう！)

 What is he doing?
（かれはなにしてるの？）

① He is throwing a ball.

 What is she doing?
（かのじょはなにしてるの？）

② She ___ sing___.

 What are you doing?
（あなたたちはなにしてるの？）

③ We ___ pull___ a rope.

 What are they doing?
（かれらはなにしてるの？）

④ They ___ study___ English.

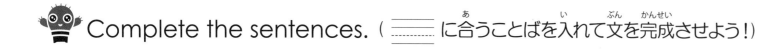 Complete the sentences. (===== に合うことばを入れて文を完成させよう！)

①  He _is_ pushing the ball.

②  She _____ touch_____ the wall.

③ 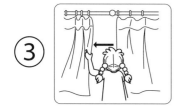 You _____ open_____ the curtains.

④  It _____ sleep_____.

⑤  They _____ play_____ soccer.

ちょっと
むずかしいけど
できるかな？

スペシャル問題!! 『動詞 + ing』にした時、動詞の形がかわるもの

【例1】 動詞の最後に『e』がつく単語は『e』をとって『ing』をつける。

write → ~~write~~ + ing → writing

➡ I am writing a letter.

【例2】 動詞の最後の文字が重なる。

run → run + n + ing → running

➡ You are running in the park.

Complete the sentences. (===== に合うことばを入れて文を完成させよう!)

① make → ~~make~~ + ing → making

➡ We _____ mak_____ a cake.

② cut → cut + t + ing → cutting

➡ She _____ cut_____ paper.

【例】 I **can** swim.
（動きを表わす）

※『できる』という意味の『can』は、動きを表わすことばと仲良しで出てくるよ!

I can cook.
（わたしは料理ができる）

I can swim.
（ぼくはおよげる）

Read the sentences. （文を読んでみよう!）

① I **can** make a cake. （わたしはケーキをつくれます。）

② I **can** play the piano. （わたしはピアノをひけます。）

③ I **can** climb a tree. （ぼくは木のぼりができます。）

④ I **can** run fast. （わたしははやく走れます。）

Write "can" on the lines. Then read the sentences and match them to the pictures.
（ _____ に『can』を入れて英文を読んだあと、文と合う絵を線で結ぼう！）

① I _____ write Japanese. •

② I _____ read English. •

③ I _____ eat noodles. •

④ I _____ cook breakfast. •

⑤ I _____ study math. •

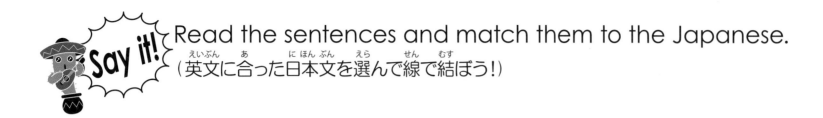

① I **can** touch a bear. •

• （ぼくは玉ねぎを食べられます。）

② I **can** eat onions. •

• （わたしは上手に歌えます。）

③ I **can** close
the window. •

• （わたしは飛べます。）

④ I **can** sing well. •

• （ぼくはくまをさわれます。）

⑤ I **can** fly. •

• （わたしはまどをしめられます。）

Choose the correct word and match the sentences to the Japanese.
(▢ から正しい英語を選んで ＝＝＝＝ に書こう！ 英文に合った日本文を選んで線で結ぼう！)

① I **can** ＿＿＿＿＿＿ the piano. •   • (ぼくは犬をあらえます。)

② I **can** ＿＿＿＿＿＿ a snake. •   • (わたしはスカイツリーに
                                                        のぼれます。)

③ I **can** ＿＿＿＿＿＿ 100 meters. •   • (わたしは 100m泳げます。)

④ I **can** ＿＿＿＿＿＿ Skytree. •   • (わたしはヘビをさわれます。)

⑤ I **can** ＿＿＿＿＿＿ a dog. •   • (わたしはピアノをひけます。)

| swim | play | climb | wash | touch |

【例】

Can you cook?

Yes, I <u>can</u>. （はい、できます。）

No, I <u>can**not**</u>. （いいえ、できません。）
（**長い形**）

No, I <u>can't</u>. （いいえ、できません。）
（**短い形**）

※P56にも出てきたように **'** マークは英語のことば を短くしてくれるよ。使い方を練習しよう！

Say it! Ask the questions to your friends and mark their answers.
（お友達に聞いてみよう！ お友達の答えの方の □ に ✔（チェック）をしよう！）

Yes, I can.　　No, I can't.

① Can you <u>swim</u>?

  □　　 □

② Can you <u>fly</u>?

  □　　 □

③ Can you <u>play</u> tennis?

  □　　 □

④ Can you <u>throw</u> a ball?

  □　　 □

Say it! Ask the questions to your friends and mark their answers.
（お友達や家族に聞いてみよう！ 聞いた相手の答えの方の ☐ に ✔ （チェック）をしよう！）

Yes, I can.　　No, I can't.

① Can you <u>drink</u> coffee?  ☐  ☐

② Can you <u>eat</u>
green peppers?  ☐  ☐

③ Can you <u>walk</u> to school?  ☐  ☐

④ Can you <u>cook</u>?  ☐  ☐

⑤ Can you <u>touch</u> a snake?  ☐  ☐

Say it! Ask the questions to your friends and mark their answers.
（お友達や家族に聞いてみよう！ 聞いた相手の答えの方の ☐ に ✔（チェック）をしよう！）

Yes, I can.　No, I can't.

① Can you <u>sleep</u> for 15 hours?  ☐　 ☐

② Can you <u>ride</u> a bike?  ☐　 ☐

③ Can you <u>run</u> fast?  ☐　 ☐

④ Can you <u>write</u> in English?  ☐　 ☐

⑤ Can you <u>make</u> a necklace?  ☐　 ☐

Say it!

Make your own questions to ask your friends.
（じぶんぶん）
（自分で文をつくってお友達や家族に聞いてみよう！）
（ともだち かぞく き）

You can use the words from the ▢.

（なか）
（ ▢ の中のことばをつかえるよ！）

Yes, I can.   No, I can't.

① Can you _____ ?   ▢   ▢

② Can you _____ ?   ▢   ▢

③ Can you _____ ?   ▢   ▢

④ Can you _____ ?   ▢   ▢

⑤ Can you _____ ?   ▢   ▢

sleep, drink, eat, swim, cook, sing, read, catch, run, climb, fly, write, throw, play

Write the correct Japanese on the lines.
（「うさぎ」はどこにいる？ 日本語の線のところに「うさぎ」のいる"ばしょ"を書いてみよう!）

Where is the rabbit?

 ⟹ It is on the hat.

うさぎはどこにいる？ ⟹ ぼうしの＿＿＿＿にいます。

 ⟹ It is in the hat.

うさぎはどこにいる？ ⟹ ぼうしの＿＿＿＿にいます。

 ⟹ It is under the hat.

うさぎはどこにいる？ ⟹ ぼうしの＿＿＿＿にいます。

on→上 / in→中 / under→下 だよ。

Say it! Look at the pictures. Choose the correct word for each picture from the ▢ and write it on the lines. Then read the sentences.

（絵を見て、それが「どこ」にあるか ▢ から選び線の上に書いてみよう！ それから英文を読んでみよう！）

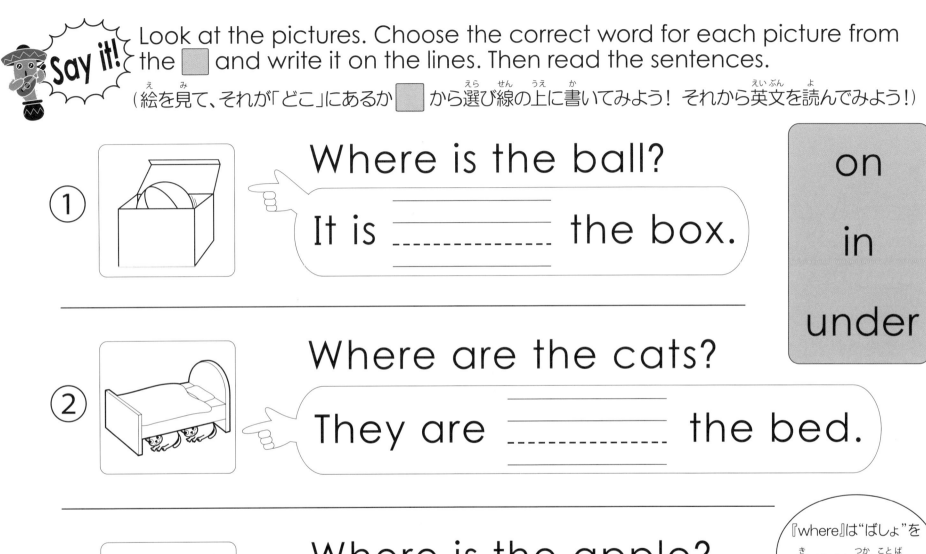

① Where is the ball?

It is _____ the box.

on

in

under

② Where are the cats?

They are _____ the bed.

③ Where is the apple?

It is _____ the table.

『where』は"ばしょ"を
聞くときに使う言葉で
"どこ？"だよ！

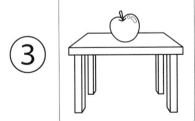

Write the correct Japanese on the lines.
(「うさぎ」はどこにいる？ 日本語の線のところに「うさぎ」のいる"ばしょ"を書いてみよう！)

 Where is the rabbit?

 ⇒ It is | by | the hat.

うさぎはどこにいる？　⇒　ぼうしの＿＿＿＿＿にいます。

 ⇒ It is | in front of | the hat.

うさぎはどこにいる？　⇒　ぼうしの＿＿＿＿＿にいます。

 ⇒ It is | between | the hats.

うさぎはどこにいる？　⇒　ぼうしの＿＿＿＿＿にいます。

by ➡ そば / in front of ➡ 前 / between ➡ 間 だよ。

Where are they? Practice writing the words on the dotted lines.

（絵を見て「みんな」はどこにいるかな？　書く練習もしようね！）

The boy is by the door.

by by

The girl is in front of the house.

in front of in front of

The fox is between the trees.

between between

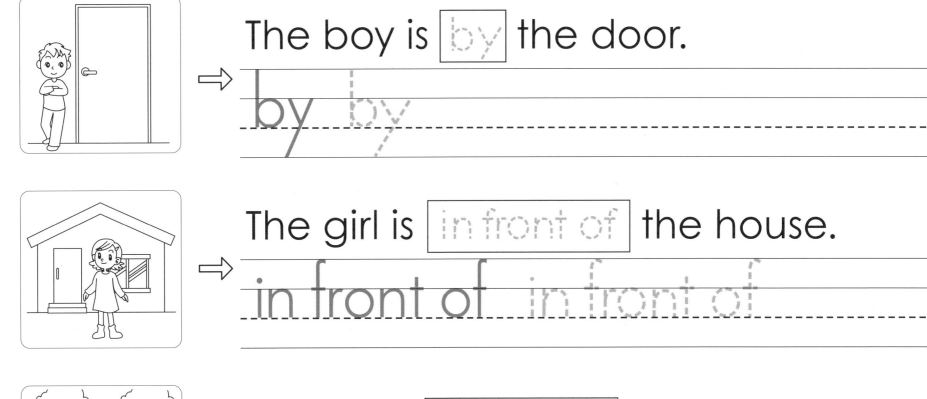

Say it! Look at the pictures. Choose the correct word for each picture from the ▨ and write it on the lines. Then read the sentences.

（絵_えを見_みて、それが「どこ」にあるか ▨ から選_{えら}び線_{せん}の上_{うえ}に書_かいてみよう！ それから英文_{えいぶん}を読_よんでみよう！）

Where is the mailbox?

① It is _____ the house.

『where』は"ばしょ"を聞_きくときに使_{つか}う言葉_{ことば}で"どこ？"だよ！

Where are the boys?

② They are _____ the rivers.

Where is the doll?

③ It is _____ the window.

by	in front of	between

Look at the pictures. Choose the correct word for each picture from the ☐ and write it on the lines. Then read the sentences.

（絵を見て、それが「どこ」にあるか ☐ から選び線の上に書いてみよう！ それから英文を読んでみよう！）

Say it!

① Where are the baskets?

They are _____ the door.

② Where is the turtle?

It is _____ the sea.

『where』は "ばしょ" を聞くとき に使う言葉で "どこ？" だよ！

③ Where is the hospital?

It is _____ the shops.

| by | in front of | between |

Look at the pictures. Choose the correct word for each picture from the ⬛ and write it on the lines. Then read the sentences.

（絵を見て、それが「どこ」にあるか ⬛ から選び線の上に書いてみよう！ それから英文を読んでみよう！）

Where are the balls?

① They are _____ the slide.

Where is the cat?

② It is _____ the table.

『where』は "ばしょ"を聞くときに 使う言葉で "どこ?"だよ！

Where are the apples?

③ They are _____ the bowl.

| on | in | under |

Say it! Let's practice using "between," "in front of" and "by."

(『between』『in front of』『by』を使って言ってみよう！)

① どこにいるの？

【例】They are between the rivers.

② どこにいるの？

It is ______________ the tree.

③ どこにいるの？

She is ______________ the mailbox.

Read the sentences.（文を読んでみよう！）

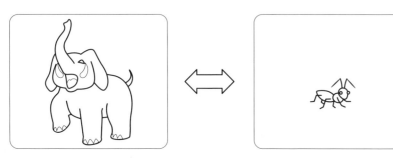

It is big.
（それは大きいです。）

It is small.
（それは小さいです。）

She is hot.
（彼女は暑いです。）

He is cold.
（彼は寒いです。）

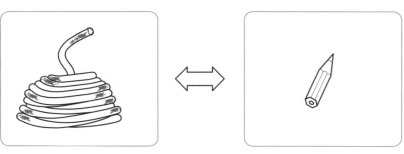

It is long.
（それは長いです。）

It is short.
（それは短いです。）

He is hungry.
（彼はおなかが空いて
　　　　います。）

She is full.
（彼女はおなかが
　　　いっぱいです。）

Write the correct Japanese in the ☐.
(のことばは人や物の"ようす"を表すことばだよ。どんな"ようす"なのか ☐ の中に日本語で書いてみよう！)

He is tall.

かれは 背が ☐ です。

He is short.

かれは 背が ☐ です。

They are clean.

They are dirty.

それらは ☐ です。

それらは ☐ です。

Write the correct Japanese in the ☐.

（ ▭ のことばは人や物の"ようす"を表すことばだよ。どんな"ようす"なのか ☐ の中に日本語で書いてみよう！）

Circle the correct word and read the sentence. （正しい英語に◯をつけ文を読んでみよう！）

①  It is (sunny / cloudy).

②  He is (tall / short).

③  It is (windy / rainy).

絵は どんなようすを 表しているかな？

④ They are (dirty / clean).

Circle the correct word and read the sentence. (正しい英語に〇をつけ文を読んでみよう!)

①  He is (tall / short).

② 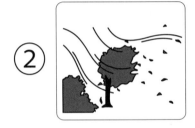 It is (windy / rainy).

③  They are (dirty / clean).

④  It is (sunny / cloudy).

絵は
どんなようすを
表しているかな?

Match the pictures to the correct words to make sentences.
（あてはまることばと線でむすぼう！）

① 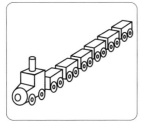 It is • • short.

②  He is • • long.

③  It is • • cold.

④  She is • • hot.

Match the pictures to the correct words to make sentences.
（あてはまることばと線でむすぼう！）

①  He is •

• tall.

②  She is •

• full.

③  He is •

• hungry.

④  I am •

• short.

Match the pictures to the correct words to make sentences.
（あてはまることばと線でむすぼう！）

①  It is　　•　　　•　big.

②  They are •　　　•　dirty.

③  It is　　•　　　•　clean.

④  They are •　　　•　small.

Write the correct words on the lines to make sentences.

（ ＿＿＿＿ にあうことばを ▢ から選んで書こう！）

① It is ＿＿＿＿＿＿＿＿＿＿＿.

②  It is ＿＿＿＿＿＿＿＿＿＿＿.

③ It is ＿＿＿＿＿＿＿＿＿＿＿.

④ It is ＿＿＿＿＿＿＿＿＿＿＿.

⑤ It is ＿＿＿＿＿＿＿＿＿＿＿.

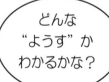
どんな
"ようす" か
わかるかな？

| long | short | sunny | big | small |

Write the correct words on the lines to make sentences.

(===== にあうことばを [   ] から選んで書こう！）

『short』は
"みじかい" にも
"ひくい" にも
使われるよ！

①  He is _____.

② She is _____.

③  He is _____.

④  He is _____.

⑤  It is _____.

| tall | short | cold | hot | rainy |

Write the correct words on the lines to make sentences.

(＿＿＿ にあうことばを ▢ から選(えら)んで書(か)こう！)

①  It is ＿＿＿＿＿＿＿＿＿.

②  She is ＿＿＿＿＿＿＿＿＿.

③ 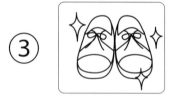 They are ＿＿＿＿＿＿＿＿＿.

④  He is ＿＿＿＿＿＿＿＿＿.

⑤ 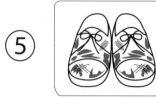 They are ＿＿＿＿＿＿＿＿＿.

dirty	clean	hungry	full	windy

Vocabulary List

nouns

a
- airplane
- alligator
- ambulance
- ant
- apple
- apron

b
- baker
- ball
- balloon
- basket
- bat
- bear
- bed
- bike
- body
- book
- bowl
- box
- boy
- breakfast
- brother
- button

c
- cake
- car
- cat
- chair
- coffee
- cook
- cow
- crab
- curry
- curtain

d
- dancer
- day
- dentist
- dish
- doctor
- dog
- doll
- door
- doughnut

e
- egg
- eggplant
- elephant
- English

f
- farmer
- fire
- firefighter
- fisherman
- flower
- fox
- friend
- frog

g
- ghost
- giraffe
- girl
- glove
- gorilla
- grape
- grasshopper
- green pepper

h
- hand
- hat
- horse
- hospital
- hour
- house

i
- igloo
- iguana
- iron

j
- Japanese
- jellyfish
- juice

k
- kangaroo
- key
- king
- kite
- koala

l
- ladder
- ladybug
- lemon
- letter
- lion
- lunch

m
- mailbox
- map
- math

m
- meter
- milk
- mouse
- music

n
- necklace
- noodle
- nurse

o
- octopus
- office worker
- onion
- orange
- owl

p
- pancake
- panda
- paper
- park
- peach
- pen
- pencil
- penguin
- pianist
- piano
- picture
- pig
- pilot
- police officer
- pool
- prince
- princess
- pumpkin

q
- queen

r
- rabbit
- riceball
- river
- rocket
- room
- rope

s
- school
- scientist
- sea
- shoe
- shop
- singer
- skeleton
- Skytree
- slide
- snake
- soccer
- soccer player
- sock
- star
- strawberry
- student

t
- table
- teacher
- tennis
- tiger
- tomato
- train
- tree
- turtle

u
- umbrella
- undershirt
- uniform

v
- vet
- violin

w
- waitress
- wall
- watch
- water
- watermelon
- window
- witch

y
- yo-yo

z
- zebra
- zookeeper

verbs

c	catch	**p**	pick
	climb		play
	close		pull
	cook		push
	cut		put
d	do	**r**	read
	draw		ride
	drink		run
e	eat	**s**	sing
f	fly		sit
g	go		sleep
h	have		stand
j	jump		study
l	like		swim
	listen	**t**	throw
	look		touch
m	make	**w**	walk
o	open		wash
			write

adjectives

b	big
c	clean
	cloudy
	cold
d	dirty
f	full
h	hot
	hungry
l	long
r	rainy
s	short
	small
	sunny
t	tall
w	windy

prepositions

a	at
b	between
	by
f	for
i	in
	in front of
o	on
t	to
u	under